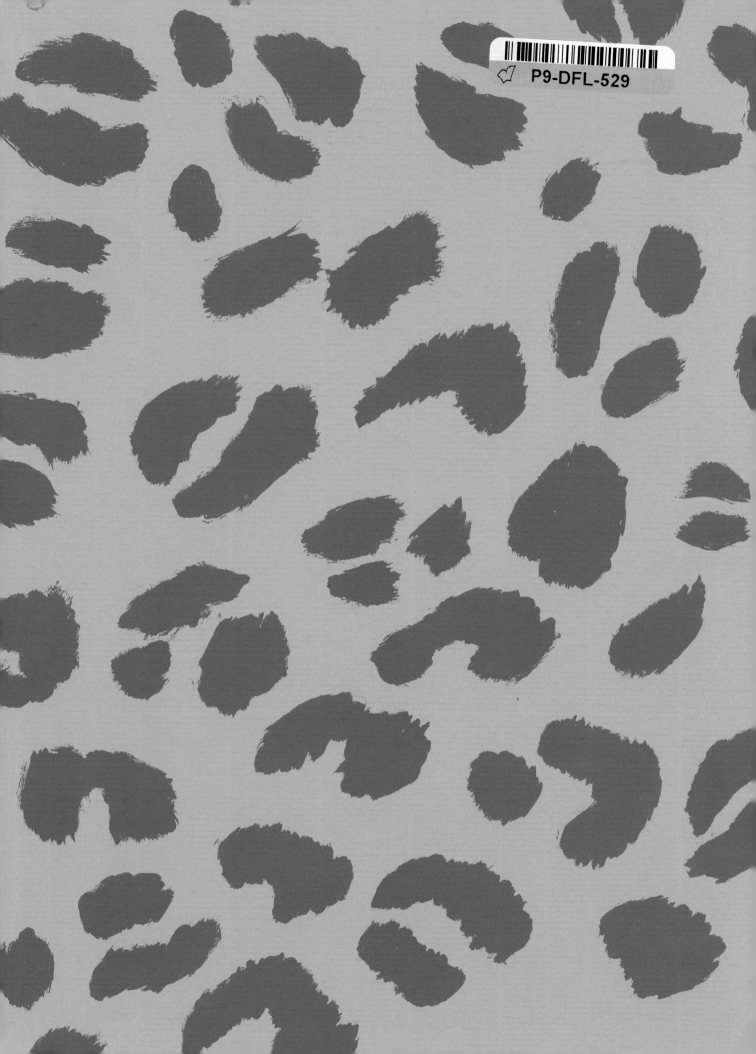

WONDERS OF THE
JUNGLE

NATIONAL WILDLIFE FEDERATION

Library of Congress CIP Data: page 95.

CONTENTS

For hundreds of years, explorers have gone into that mysterious green tangle we call the jungle. Some went because of tales of gold, of great cities, and of strange peoples. Others went just because jungles were full of mystery. Some came out of the jungles with stories of incredible dangers and hardships. Some told of amazing animals and of lands of beauty beyond belief. Others never came out of the jungles at all.

Even today the jungle is a mysterious place, and it can be dangerous. But scientists see the jungle as a frontier where they can discover animals and plants no explorer has ever seen before. And some jungles are still frontiers. Scientists first explored some unknown jungles of New Guinea in 1959 at the same time spacecraft charted the unknown far side of the moon.

Now, people by the millions are moving into the jungle. They go there to mine its gold, harvest its timber, and farm its land. Each year there is less and less wild land left. But there are still some jungles in this world filled with mysteries that challenge us to explore and study.

WHAT ARE JUNGLES . . .

What do you see when you try to imagine a jungle? A hot, steamy forest cluttered with strange, noisy animals and tangled vines? That is how many people think of it. And some jungles are like that in certain places and at certain times of day. But not all jungles are alike, and each kind has a different name.

Most jungles are what scientists call *tropical rain forests*. The word *tropical* refers to the part of the earth that lies along the equator. The tropics extend about 1,600 miles north and 1,600 miles south of the equator.

The tropics are different from other parts of the world. Outside the tropics, days are long in the summer and short in the winter. That is caused by the way the earth tilts on its axis as it revolves around the sun. But as you get closer to the equator,

the earth's tilt makes less difference. In the tropics, days are never much longer than thirteen hours or shorter than eleven.

The steady flow of sunshine keeps tropical rain forests warm all year round. The temperature in Kansas may average 82°F in July and only 31°F in January. The temperature in a tropical rain forest may drop from 83°F in "summer" months to 80°F in "winter" months—almost no change.

And there is nearly always moisture in the tropical rain forest. Rain may not fall every day, but the ground rarely dries out. A tropical rain forest may get as much rain in a month as Seattle, Washington, gets in a year—more than three feet of water. And Seattle is famous in the United States for all its rain!

Rain forests aren't the only kind of jungle in the tropics. There are *trop-*

Dripping from a jungle rain, a Central American sloth (right) looks green because tiny plants called *algae* grow on its damp fur.

A colorful toucan (far right) stands out in the leafy green of the forest. This bird uses its large but light beak to pick up berries, eggs, and insects to eat.

... AND WHERE ARE THEY?

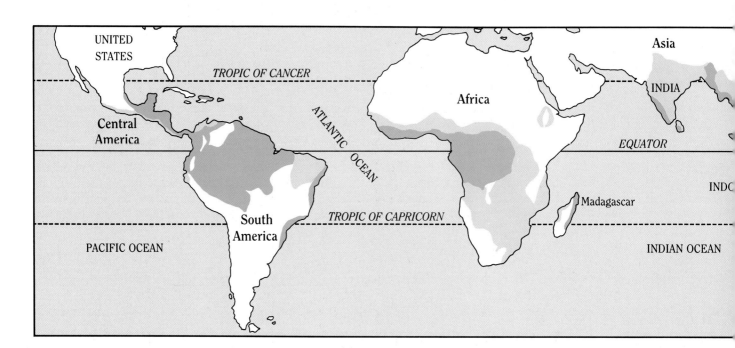

UNITED
STATES

TROPIC OF CANCER

Central
America

ATLANTIC OCEAN

South
America

TROPIC OF CAPRICORN

PACIFIC OCEAN

Africa

Asia

INDIA

EQUATOR

INDO

Madagascar

INDIAN OCEAN

Rain forests appear in dark green on the map above. Seasonal forests appear in light green. Both kinds of forest are called *jungles*. The two dotted lines mark the northern and southern edges of the tropics.

ical seasonal forests, too. Their "seasons" are not hot and cold months, but wet and dry ones. And in many places, mile after mile of *cloud forest* stretch across the mountains. These jungles are kept wet both by rain and by mists and clouds.

Seen from above, jungles look like a sea of solid green. And to many people, that's what jungles must be like all the way through. They think travelers have to hack through jungles with a machete, inch by inch.

The tops of the trees, where the sun beats down, do form an almost solid umbrella. And where a river cuts through the jungle and lets in sunlight, the greenery spreads all the way from the treetops to the ground. But walk deep inside the jungle, and you're in a different place.

It may take a while to get used to the strange, dim, green light. The

branches overhead block ninety percent of the sunlight. In fact, it's hard to tell just where the sun is.

As your eyes adjust to the dimness, you realize that the interior of the jungle isn't at all like you imagined. Without much light, plants can't grow very well. In many places, you have a lot of room to walk. The ground is covered only by ferns, seedlings, fungi, and a thin carpet of fallen leaves and flowers.

Listen. Do you hear anything? If it's the middle of the day, you will probably hear very little. Birds and other animals are usually most active and noisy at dawn and dusk.

Take a deep breath. The air has that special smell that comes along before a rainstorm.

Also, the jungle probably is not as hot as you thought it would be. Though the air is warm, it's almost

Philippines

Borneo

New Guinea

AUSTRALIA

always cooler than it is in Kansas City or Chicago in July.

Where are these jungles? When they hear the world *jungle,* many people automatically think of Africa. They *should* think of Latin America. The largest jungle area in the world is in South America. Most of the tropical forests there are in Brazil, but some of them extend northward through Central America to Mexico.

The main part of the African jungle lies along the equator. Much of this jungle surrounds the Zaire River, but other sections stretch westward to the Atlantic coast. A strip of jungle also grows along the east coast of the

continent and on Madagascar, an island just east of Africa.

Asia's jungles are really widespread. Most of India's jungles are seasonal forests, but patches of rain forest grow there and from Burma to Singapore. Throughout this hot region, islands—Sumatra, Borneo, New Guinea, the Philippines, and more—have jungles. Australia has a narrow fringe on its northeast coast.

These jungles are incredibly rich in wildlife. Tropical rain forests alone may cover only one-twelfth of the earth's lands. But they are home to more than half of all the types of animals and plants known to man.

Strangely shaped trees and soft, filtered light give the lush Latin American jungle at right a look of mystery.

LIFE IN THE TREES

THE UMBRELLAS

The jungle is made up of trees. *Lots* of trees. Just one square mile of *tropical rain forest* jungle may have several hundred kinds of trees. That's twenty or thirty times the variety of a square mile of woods outside the tropics.

The jungles' trees compete with each other for sunlight. The trees that get the most sunlight grow the tallest. The ones that get less sunlight don't grow as tall. On most tropical rain forest trees, the branches grow near the very top, spreading out to let the leaves get as much sunlight as possible. The different heights of these trees form layers, and some of them have special names.

The *understory* is formed by short trees and the shrubs and bushes that grow near the ground. Taller trees' branches spread out and make a thick layer, called the *canopy,* which acts almost like an umbrella over the understory. Here and there pokes through a super-tall tree—called an *emergent* because it emerges from the canopy. When the tall trees die and fall, they leave openings in the canopy where light shines through. Some of the shorter trees that were unable to get much sunlight before start growing upward into the top layer.

In the United States, a white pine grows less than a foot and a half a year. But the steady light and warmth of the tropics help trees there grow quickly. In Asia, a type of tree related to beans and peas grows about a foot a month. One kind of tropical Asian bamboo, which is really a grass rather

Perched more than 100 feet above the jungle floor, the scientist at left studies life in the hidden world of the tropical treetops.

Clouds sweeping across the trees bring moisture to a Costa Rican cloud forest (above). In some jungles, a rain can bring twenty times as much water as a shower outside the tropics.

than a tree, grows nearly two feet a *day* until it reaches its maximum height of 100 feet.

The taller rain forest trees form a leafy roof that blocks out the sunlight that would heat up and dry out the ground. As a result, in most places the forest floor is not bright or hot like the canopy, and the humidity is always high. When storms blow overhead, the treetops swing, but the canopy keeps most of the wind from reaching the ground. A person on the ground feels only a breeze.

Heavy rains beat down on the canopy. The raindrops splatter on the leaves and run off their pointed tips, called *drip tips*. The rain reaches the ground as a soft mist. Because the water drains right off, the leaves dry quickly. Fungi and other things harmful to the leaves find it harder to grow on them.

13

Tall, solid buttresses (above) and long, round stilt roots (above right) help hold up trees whose shallow roots grow in thin soil.

The large variety of trees also helps keep the tropical rain forest healthy. Because the tropics are filled with plant diseases and plant eaters, it wouldn't take much for an epidemic to destroy a forest—if the trees were all the same kind. But because there are so many different kinds of trees, if one kind of tree dies, others will fill the space it leaves.

Some rain forest trees have unusual trunks and roots. The trunks of some trees stick out like the fins at the base of a rocket. The fin-shaped parts of the tree trunk are called *buttresses*. The widest portion sticks out several feet from the tree's base.

Some buttresses are two or three times as tall as a grown person. A few kinds of trees have as many as ten buttresses each.

The trunks of other trees end in strange roots that look like giant stilts. They stick out from the tree's trunk, then curve down into the soil like hundreds of hungry fingers soaking up nutrients and water.

What are these strange buttresses and stilt roots for? Scientists think that they help support the trees, whose regular roots may be very shallow. These supports help keep the trees from falling over when they are pounded by tropical storms.

14

TARZAN'S VINES

In the movies, Tarzan makes his way through the jungle by swinging from one thick vine to another. These vines are called *lianas* (lee-AH-nuhs), a word that refers to all hanging vines, not just a single kind. Lianas twist almost magically upward and disappear in the green maze of the treetops. Some lianas climb one tree, drop back down to the ground, and grow up another tree.

Because there are so many lianas, Tarzan can travel just about anywhere he wants without having to land on the ground and walk to the next vine. And he doesn't have to worry that the liana might break under his weight. Some lianas weigh more than a ton, and the added weight of a person would make little difference.

So many lianas grow in the jungle that they tie the tops of the trees together. If a tree dies or is cut, the lianas may keep it from falling. Foresters sometimes have to cut a whole group of trees before the one they want will come down.

Lianas do more than hold up dead trees. A few kinds of liana provide drinking water for thirsty people. All a person has to do is cut through a vine, and out pours pure water to drink. But he had better be sure he's cutting the right kind of vine. The water in some lianas is poisonous.

OUT ON A LIMB

The South American uakari (left) looks like a devil, but this monkey is really gentle. It spends its days picking fruit in the trees.

Large eyes enable India's slender lorises (below) and Africa's bush baby (bottom) to see the insects they hunt in trees at night.

Where are all the animals? Visitors to the jungle often ask this question. They listen and look, but they hear little and see even less. The problem is knowing where to look. Most jungle animals aren't on the ground at all. They are up in the trees—out on limbs and often out of sight.

Many of these tree creatures are insects (see pages 38-41). Many are colorful birds (see pages 28-33). And many are the warm-blooded, furry creatures called *mammals.*

One of the big problems for mammals living in trees is to keep from falling. Uakaris in South America, lorises in Asia, and bush babies in Africa—all have long toes that wrap around tree limbs and keep them from falling. These mammals are

Some treetop animals, like spider monkeys (below) and the prehensile-tailed porcupine (below left), use strong tails to hold on as they move along thin limbs.

primates. Like most primates, they also have hands that can grasp things. Their feet and hands are a lot like human hands, which is not surprising since people, too, are primates.

Other mammals have prehensile (pree-HEN-sill) tails that help them keep from falling. These tails are long and very strong, and can be used like hands. As the animals travel through the trees, they grasp branches with their hands, feet, *and* tails.

Monkeys live in jungles all around the world. Almost all monkeys have long tails. But not all long tails are prehensile and can be used like hands. A few kinds of monkeys in Latin America have prehensile tails. Spider monkeys, for example, can use their tails to pick things up as well as to hang on to branches. But most monkeys, including all monkeys in Asia and Africa, can only use their tails for balance when they run or jump.

Claws are another tool that some tree-dwelling mammals have. The South American tamandua (tuh-MAN-dew-uh), or "lesser anteater," has a prehensile tail and strong claws. These claws help the tamandua both in climbing and in getting food. It wraps its tail around tree limbs to hold on while it rips open ant and termite nests with its claws. The

By using its tail to grip the tree's trunk, a tamandua (right) leaves the claws on its front feet free to rip open a termite nest for food.

About the size of a large house cat, the South American margay (above) hunts mainly in trees. It easily climbs and jumps among the branches, pouncing on its prey of birds and small mammals.

tamandua's neighbor, the prehensile-tailed porcupine, hangs on the same way. But this little creature uses its claws mainly for climbing. Sloths don't have prehensile tails, but do have long, curved claws that circle branches. Sloth's claws hold on to branches so well that the animals eat, mate, and have young while hanging upside down.

Some people think that the best climbers and acrobats in the jungle are the gibbons. These apes live in Asia, from the island of Borneo to China. Gibbons have extra-long arms. When they swing from branch to branch, they cover nearly 10 feet in one swing. They are so skillful that when they leap they can even catch birds in midair.

Some of the world's rarest apes, the orangutans, also make their forest homes on Borneo and Sumatra.

Orangutans are the only other apes that spend most of their lives in trees. Like the gibbons, they swing on long arms. They also use hook-shaped hands and feet for grasping branches.

Mammals that live in trees are usually safe from tigers and other cats that hunt in jungles from time to time (see pages 64-67). But a South American cat called the *margay* seems to spend a lot of time up in the trees. These house-cat-sized creatures are rare, and not much is known about their life in the wild. Scientists think they hunt by night for birds, tree frogs, lizards, and other animals.

There may be many animals on the highest branches that we know nothing about. Scientists call the jungle treetops "the last great frontier of biology." In the past, explorers mapped new lands. Now they must map a world high in the treetops.

20

The gibbon (below) has arms twice as long as its body. It uses them to travel hand-over-hand and to reach food—fruit and leaves—at the ends of branches.

A mother orangutan (below) will usually build a new nest in the trees every night for herself and her young.

A baby sloth finds it easy to rest, sleep, and nurse as its mother hangs upside-down.

PIGGYBACK PLANTS

These colorful plants are epiphytes, special kinds of plants that grow on high limbs of trees where they can get the light they need.

Small plants in the jungle have a problem. Many of them don't grow well on the ground because it's too dark. They can't grow tall like trees and push their way up through the forest to reach the light. So what do some of them do? They grow on the trees' high branches, where light does shine through.

Plants that grow on trees this way are called *epiphytes* (EPP-ih-fites).

The name means "upon plants." You could say that epiphytes ride piggyback on the trees.

An epiphyte begins life as a seed dropped by a bird or other animal or blown by the wind. The seed sticks on rough bark or lands in a notch on a tree limb. The best spot is where a little patch of soil has been created by rotted leaves. Rains keep the soil wet, and soon the seed sprouts. The tree on which an epiphyte grows is called a *host*.

Many jungle plants grow this way: orchids, bromeliads (broe-ME-lih-ads) mosses, ferns, and even shrubs and small trees. Orchids have some of the most colorful flowers. But among the most unusual epiphytes are bromeliads, relatives of pineapples.

Some bromeliads make a small world all their own. Their leaves form cups that catch and hold fresh rainwater, as much as two gallons or more. These cups are called *bromeliad tanks*. Worms and beetles and creatures too small to see live in the tanks. Frogs and salamanders may also live there, and small mammals wander by to nibble on insects.

Bromeliads and other epiphytes can be a real burden for a host tree to carry. They may take minerals from the rainwater before it splashes down to the tree's roots. They may block the light that the tree's leaves need to grow. And sometimes they make the tree top-heavy. Top-heavy trees are much more likely to be blown down in a storm.

But trees don't take this burden standing still—so to speak. The bark of some trees is smooth. The result is that seeds don't have a good place to stick and start growing. On some trees, the bark is poisonous and keeps any seeds on it from sprouting. And other trees shed their bark. When the bark falls, so do the epiphytes growing on it. Did the trees develop smooth or poisonous bark just to keep epiphytes off? Probably not. But

this is a puzzle that scientists are trying to solve.

Now scientists think that some epiphytes really help the host trees. True, the epiphytes take some food, water, and light that the tree needs. But the tree may get it all back—and more. When epiphytes die, they fall to the ground, rot, and turn into food for the tree's roots. The falling epiphytes also carry animal droppings

and the bodies of dead insects and other jungle creatures. These also decay and become part of the soil that feeds the host tree.

Some trees don't wait for the epiphytes to fall off. Instead, the trees grow roots up on their branches where the epiphytes are. These branch roots poke into the soil under the epiphytes and absorb food the tree might otherwise miss.

A pool of water in a bromeliad plant makes a safe place for this pygmy marsupial frog to release a tadpole.

THE STRANGLERS

This may sound like a horror story. A guest arrives for a visit and refuses to leave. Gradually the guest takes over the living room, the dining room, then the kitchen. By the end of the story, the guest has taken over the entire house. The owners have been killed. Is this a fantasy? Not really. Something like it happens every day in jungles.

The guest is a type of plant called a *strangler*. There are many kinds of strangler plants. In Latin America, one of them is a fig called *matapalo* (matt-ah-PAHL-oh), which means "tree killer." It begins life as an epiphyte, growing high on the branches of a tree. The house that the strangler fig takes over is the host tree where it starts growing.

The strangler's story begins when a bird or bat drops a fig seed in the top of a tree. The seed sprouts, perhaps in a hollow in branches where water and soil have collected. Most jungle epiphytes start life in just this way, but few grow to be big trees.

A strangler fig grows slowly, but it never stops growing. First, it sends roots down to the ground. Some of these roots hang down in the air until they anchor themselves in the ground. Other roots creep down along the trunk of the host tree. Sometimes the fig's roots grow to be more than 90 feet long.

When the roots reach the ground, they absorb more water and nutrients, and the fig starts growing faster. As it spreads out through the top of its host tree, its leaves rob the host of the light it needs. The fig's roots encircling the host tree's trunk also become longer and thicker. And where they touch, they grow together. Often the host tree finally dies and rots away. The strangler fig is left standing as a new, hollow tree.

But this story has a happy ending. Yes, the strangler fig kills its host. But it feeds and shelters many of the jungle's animals. Birds, bats, and monkeys eat the tasty figs right off the fig tree. Peccaries—distant relatives of pigs—and other creatures feed on figs that fall to the ground.

Where the fig's roots have grown together, deep grooves make safe homes for many small creatures. During the day, geckos—colorful lizards—scramble from the grooves to feed and to fight for mates. Elsewhere on the tree, male anole lizards flash their pink and purple throat skin to court mates. Sometimes these displays attract predators that want to eat the lizards. But the lizards quickly dash back into the protective grooves and are safe for another day.

Paper wasps also build nests in the safety of these deep grooves. They post guards to fight off ants and other creatures that come too close to their nest. Nearby, stingless bees chew their way into the hollow left by the dead and decayed host tree. Some bee colonies stay with a fig tree until it, too, dies and falls down.

During the night, whip scorpions explore the fig tree's wrinkled trunk. These two-inch-long relatives of both scorpions and spiders grab roaches,

After sprouting in a notch in a tree (above), a strangler fig sends down roots that surround the tree's trunk (right). The fig becomes a new, hollow tree when the tree it surrounds dies and rots away (far right).

crickets, and other tasty prey. Spiders weave their silky traps across the fig's roots. And snails, millipedes, and centipedes wander up from the forest floor. In the high branches, bats take off on their nightly rounds.

The strangler fig began as a simple sprout in a high hollow. It turned into a killer. But it ended as a welcome source of food and shelter for creatures of all sizes.

FANCY FEATHERS

From Asia to Africa to Latin America, jungles are incredibly rich in bird life. Nearly a third of the world's bird species are found only in the jungles. Many others spend their winters there. Scientists once counted the birds in a Costa Rican jungle preserve barely half the size of tiny Rhode Island. They found a greater variety there than in all of North America.

The most famous jungle birds are parrots. Green, blue, red, yellow, orange—parrots hardly miss a color in their bright feathers. Some, like the golden parakeet and hyacinth macaw, have only one or two colors. Others, like the scarlet macaw, have nearly every color of the rainbow.

Parrots climb trees almost as well as they fly. This ability is useful in the dense canopy, where flying can be difficult. The birds push and pull themselves up with their sharp beaks and strong claws.

Some parrots use their feet to hold nuts and other food while they eat.

South America's green-winged macaw (right) is one of the most colorful parrots in the tropics. It was named for the green feathers, hard to see here, on the other side of its wings.

Asia's rhinoceros hornbill (below) may use its giant beak to fight other birds or to knock down fruit to eat.

Mayan and Aztec Indians once worshipped the quetzal (above). Today the bird is pictured on money and stamps in Guatemala.

Spotted feathers allow
greater potoos (POE-
toos) to blend into the
background on light-
colored trees. Can you
see *both* birds here?

The birds' hooked beaks are built for
cracking hard nuts, but they are just
as useful for nibbling on fruit. A
parrot's beak is strong enough to cut
through the thin wire of bird cages.

Toucans rival the parrots for col-
or—but they are best known for their
large beaks. Some toucans have beaks
longer than the rest of their bodies.
These colorful South American birds
eat fruit, berries, insects, and even
birds' eggs and nestlings.

The jungles of Africa and Asia
shelter other kinds of large-billed
birds, the hornbills. A large, bony
tube grows on top of many of these
birds' beaks. Called a *casque,* the tube
probably works like an echo chamber
to make the calls louder.

Some jungle birds are so beautiful
that the Europeans who first saw
them said they came from Paradise.
These are the so-called birds of paradise. They live only in northern
Australia, New Guinea, and a few
nearby islands. Some grow long, colorful tail plumes. Others sprout
bright, strange-shaped feathers from
their heads. But only the males are so
colorful. They use their feathers to
show off and attract their drab, dull-
colored mates.

Male blue birds of paradise, and
several others, are not content with
just sitting and calling. They court
females by hanging upside down so
their bright tail feathers spread out
like lacy fans.

Long, colorful feathers helped
make the quetzal (KETT-sull) an offi-
cial bird of some Latin American

CHANGING COLORS

Like the ruby topaz hummingbird (below), some jungle birds have feathers that flash brightly in the sunlight and change color as the birds move. This flashing, changing color is called *iridescence.*

Usually, colors are created by chemicals called *pigments.* Pigments make up the colors in paint, skin, leaves, and most feathers. These colors stay the same no matter how you look at them. But iridescent colors are created by the way light is reflected from the top and bottom surfaces of very thin, clear objects —like soap bubbles, films of oil on water, and the coatings on some bird feathers. As the objects move, the reflections of the light change and so do the colors they make.

To attract mates and drive away other males, the Emperor bird of paradise spreads its feathers and, sometimes, flips over to hang upside down.

royalty. Mayan and Aztec Indians thought these birds were gods. Aztec noblemen used the two-foot-long, green tail feathers of the quetzal on ceremonial clothing. The Central American nation of Guatemala still honors the quetzal by using it as the country's symbol.

Throughout jungles, tiny birds of many kinds fly from limb to limb. Most of these birds have short, broad wings that are very useful in flying in and out of places where there is little room to move around.

Many of these small birds feed on insects. The flycatchers sit quietly on limbs, then dart out to nab their

meals in midair. Different kinds of antbirds follow the army ants marching through the underbrush. They're not after the ants, though. They want the spiders, insects, and other small animals that come out of hiding to escape the ants.

Day and night, sharp-clawed and keen-eyed birds of prey search from the canopy down to the jungle floor. Among these hunters are the largest eagles in the world.

Harpy eagles, the largest ones anywhere, live in the Amazon jungle in South America. They sometimes grab monkeys and sloths right off the trees, and may even chase other animals on the ground. Philippine eagles in Asia and crowned eagles in Africa are smaller, but just as deadly. All these eagles hunt during the day.

Not all jungle birds are large or unusual. Some look ordinary and familiar. And they ought to. These are the same birds that spend the summers in North America, then return south to the tropics for the winter. Warblers, tanagers, vireos, and others are as much at home in the jungles of Latin America during our winter as they are in the woodlands of the United States in our summer.

Now many birds return to the tropics only to find that their jungle homes have been cut down—maybe to clear the way for a road or a farm. As a result, they have no place to live and find food during our winter. Fewer and fewer birds each year come back north to find mates, build nests, and raise families.

The Philippine eagle is an excellent hunter. It can even kill and eat poisonous cobra snakes. But despite the bird's common name, monkey-eating eagle, it rarely attacks monkeys.

32

THE GLIDERS

The jungle treetops are full of surprises. People expect to see parrots and other birds flying from tree to tree. The surprise comes when some odd-looking "bird" turns out to be a frog—or a snake.

This is no trick of the imagination. Some jungle snakes, lizards, frogs, squirrels and other creatures are able to "fly." They don't fly the way birds do, by flapping wings or soaring on rising columns of warm air. Instead, they spread out some part of their bodies to glide downward, a lot like leaves falling gently in the breeze. Gliding helps them get away from predators and also helps them chase their own prey.

Flying squirrels are the most common gliders in many regions. These animals even live in Canada and the United States, where there are no jungles. Furry flaps of skin stretch out along their sides from their arms down to their legs. When the squirrels leap, these flaps trap air like the wings of hang gliders.

The biggest flying squirrels live in Southeast Asia. They are the size of house cats, with tails more than two feet long. One of them was seen gliding a quarter of a mile.

Asian flying lemurs and Australian pygmy gliding possums have skin flaps and glide the way flying squirrels do. When they land on branches, they dig in with sharp claws to keep from falling off. Females also use their flaps as cradles for their young.

Flying snakes, also from Southeast Asia, don't have skin flaps to help

Skin flaps act like wings for the flying gecko (below) and the flying lemur (right). A flying lemur mother also uses her flaps to cradle her youngster (below right).

them glide. They swivel their ribs so their bodies are thin and wide instead of tubular. When their bodies are spread out, they float downward on a cushion of air.

When Asia's flying tree frogs leap from branches, they spread the toes of their wide, webbed feet to make mini-parachutes. By moving their legs or twisting their toes, they can change direction to land just where they want to.

One scientist calls the flying dragon "the most accomplished of all the gliding animals." This *dragon* is really a lizard about eight to ten inches long. As it glides, the flying dragon uses moveable ribs to stretch out colorful flaps of skin along its sides. But the lizard doesn't float straight down. It uses strong muscles in its skin flaps to adjust the flaps' shape and change its direction.

35

BATS! BATS! BATS!

White tent bats (below) make snug homes by bending leaves so that they cover the bats like a tent. These six bats together weigh about one ounce.

When darkness comes, most of the birds become quiet. It's time for them to rest. But the jungle skies are still busy, for early evening and night is the time of the bats.

During the day, giant Asian bats called "flying foxes" usually hang from jungle trees like fruit. Their foxlike faces give them their common name. But other animals have nothing to fear from these "foxes." Flying foxes eat fruit, not meat.

Many kinds of bats visit jungle flowers, lapping up the sugary nectar and spreading pollen from flower to flower in the process. Flowers of the trees that are visited by bats tend to be light-colored. That makes them easier to see in the dark when the bats are out feeding. Some tropical trees, like the durian and baobab, depend on bats to spread their pollen and fertilize them.

These fruit-eating and nectar-drinking bats also use smell to find their food. Fortunately, the plants that need the bats give off odors that are hard to miss. One tree in Asia opens its scented flowers around ten o'clock at night. By midnight the smell of the flowers is so strong—and so bad—that the tree is called "the midnight horror."

Many bats—both in the jungles and elsewhere—eat insects. They find their prey with sound. First, they send out high-pitched squeaks. Then their ears pick up the echoes as the squeaks bounce off the prey. This is called *echolocation.* Bats also use

Both the white tent bat (bottom) and the tube-nosed bat (below) eat fruit. The fringed-lipped bat (below right) eats insects and lizards, but prefers frogs.

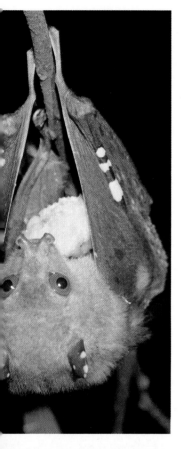

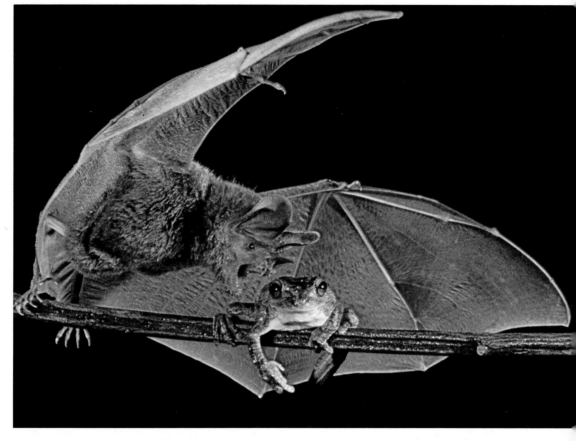

echoes to detect obstacles and avoid going *bump!* in the night.

Mention bats to some people and their first thought is of vampire bats. Blood-lapping vampire bats do range through the jungles of Central and South America. But they are usually more interested in other mammals than in people.

Fascinating as the vampires may seem to us, many other kinds of bats are equally interesting. Among these are Latin America's frog-eating bats, which have a reputation for being superb hunters. Hunting at night, they fly straight to the ponds where frogs gather to find mates. Once

there, the bats listen for the whines and chirps of the frogs' mating calls. The bats can tell the difference between the calls of edible frogs and poisonous frogs. The bats can also tell by sound which frogs are too large for them to eat.

The jungles—and people, too —need bats. Some bats pollinate flowers. Some spread seeds when they eat fruit and leave their seed-filled droppings elsewhere. Some of these seeds grow into plants, and thus the bats help keep the jungle alive. Other bats eat harmful insects. As one scientist puts it, all bats "deserve much more respect and consideration."

SMALL
BUT MIGHTY

Most jungle animals are smaller than your hand. That may seem hard to believe when you think about monkeys, tigers, and other large animals. But don't forget. Tiny insects and the like are animals too—and the jungles' trees are filled with an amazing variety of these creatures.

If you were in a jungle, you wouldn't have to look very hard to find insects and other tiny animals. They would find you. Mosquitoes, ants, ticks, chiggers—all kinds of biting and stinging creatures—can make life miserable for people in the jungle. They are annoying when they attack, and some are also dangerous. Some mosquitoes carry diseases like malaria and yellow fever. Some of the flies spread worms that grow in the bloodstreams of the people they bite.

Some people say that the worst pests are ants, especially when they crawl over people and start biting. But these tiny creatures are fascinating to watch and to study.

Tailor ants work like human tailors, sewing leaves together with silk threads. First, some of the ants crawl over leaves and pull the edges together. Then come ants carrying ant larvae. The larvae give off a sticky silk. As the ants carrying the larvae walk back and forth from one leaf to another, the larvae's sticky silk "stitches" the leaves together. Soon the ants have built a nest of leaves.

Other kinds of ants act like partners with jungle plants. The best-known partnership is with some kinds

In a tailor ant nest (above), everyone works—even the youngsters. Adults carry the young back and forth across the edges of leaves (right). Silk made by the young glues the leaves together to form a nest.

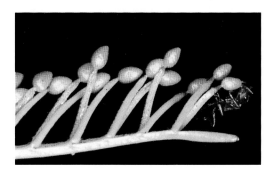

of acacia (uh-KAY-shuh) trees. These feathery-leaved members of the pea family can be found in seasonal jungles as well as outside jungles.

These "ant" acacias have hollow thorns in which the ants live. The ants patrol the trees, ready to attack whatever creatures land there.

Ants protect acacias from other plants, too. They chew up vines that try to climb the acacia trees. And they may even keep all other plants trimmed back for several feet around.

In return for their protection, the ants get food as well as a place to live. They eat special pods that grow on the acacia's leaves. They also drink nectar produced in special glands at the base of the leaves.

This partnership is not only useful, it is also necessary. A scientist once took all the ants off some acacias. Without their ants, the trees were soon killed by insects and other leaf-eaters. The scientist then tried raising the ants away from acacia trees. Without their special acacia food, the ants also died.

Some insects are tough enough to get past these ant guards. In Costa Rica, shiny green ant-acacia beetles nibble on acacia leaves even while ants crawl all over them. The beetles succeed where other insects fail because they are protected by strong armor that ants cannot bite through.

Strong armor has also helped beetles survive everywhere to become the most successful group of insects in the world. How many kinds of beetles are there? Scientists guess at

Bullhorn acacia trees (above) provide both a home and food for ants. Ants live in the trees' hollow thorns (top right) and eat **special food that grows on the leaves (top left). In return, the ants attack insects and other creatures that try to eat the trees' leaves.**

Stinging hairs protect
the silkmoth caterpillar
(below) from hungry
birds and other preda-
tors. The bright gold
beetle (bottom) is
shielded from enemies
by its thick shell.

Leafhoppers (right)
hang upside down when
they poke their
mouthparts into plants.
Water and nutrients
moving up from the
plant's roots flow right
into their bodies.

least 500,000—and there are probably
many more! In Panama, scientists
studying one kind of tree found more
than 1,200 kinds of beetles on it.

Leafhoppers are another successful
group of insects that live in jungles.
There are about 5,000 kinds of leafhoppers, including those in the jungles and elsewhere.

Most leafhoppers are small. Even
the largest ones measure barely half
an inch long. When large numbers of
leafhoppers gather on plants to feed,
they can do a lot of harm. They drill
holes in the stems of plants to tap the
water and nutrients inside them.
Sometimes they take so much that
the plants wilt. They may even poke
so many holes that the plants never
recover. And sometimes they carry
deadly viruses that kill the plants.

Though they sometimes harm
plants, leafhoppers can be useful to
other small creatures. When
leafhoppers drink more nutrients than
they can use, the extra liquid passes
through their bodies and becomes
"honeydew," which other insects eat.

Caterpillars that live in jungles
have leaves to eat all year round.
Outside the tropics, caterpillars usually appear just once a year, when
there are plenty of young, tender
leaves to eat. After a season of eating,
they form pupae and often make cocoons and spend the winter in them.
They emerge the next year as adult
moths or butterflies. But in jungles
without long dry seasons, caterpillars
and their adult forms can be found
any time of the year.

Jungle Disguises

Not everything in the jungle is what it seems to be. The objects above look like a colorful orchid and a damaged leaf. But look closer. They are both insects in disguise. The "orchid" is really a Malaysian flower mantis. Its disguise helps it get food. When an insect doesn't see the mantis and lands nearby, the mantis snags it for dinner. The "leaf" is an Amazonian katydid. Its disguise helps it hide from insect-eating creatures. They will pass right by this katydid, thinking it is just another leaf.

HIGH-UP HOPPERS

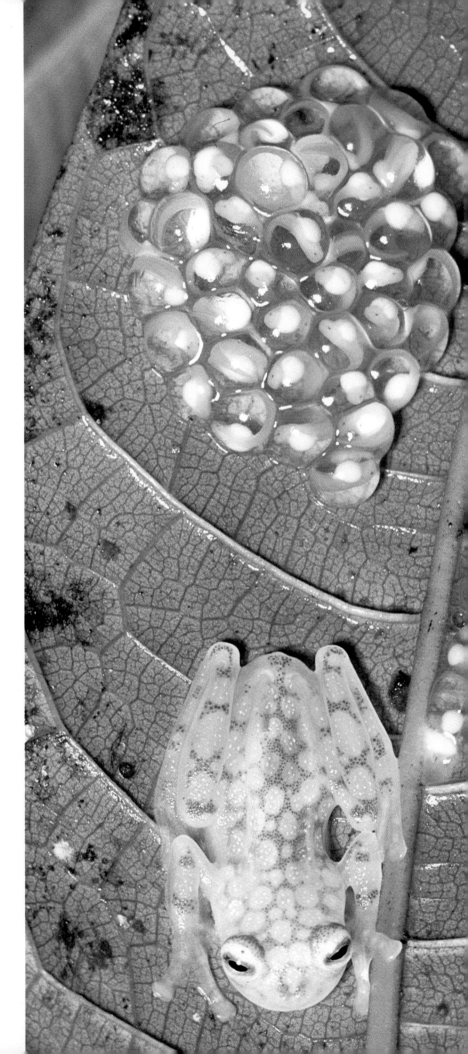

Scientists knew that the frogs were there. They could hear the males singing loudly through the jungle, calling for mates. But they also knew better than to look for the creatures only around marshes or streams, places you would usually expect to find frogs. These frogs were hiding in the trees. Some were a hundred feet over the peoples' heads.

At least half of the jungles' frogs live in the trees. Like frogs everywhere, jungle frogs like wet places. The jungles have many marshes, ponds, and streams. But there are not as many tadpoles and frogs in them as you might expect. Why not? Many fish and insects live in these bodies of water. The fish and insects like to eat frogs' eggs and tadpoles. That is why jungle frogs often look elsewhere for safe places to lay their eggs.

Some frogs don't climb far up into the trees. They lay their eggs on leaves that hang low over water. When the eggs hatch, the tadpoles plop into the water and swim away.

Marsupial tree frogs take no chances with their eggs. The females let the eggs develop in pouches on their backs. One kind of marsupial frog keeps about 20 eggs in its pouch. It holds them there until they develop into young frogs. Another kind keeps as many as 200 eggs at a time. But once these eggs hatch, the parent drops the tadpoles into a puddle of rainwater where they can grow.

Some of the Asian tree frogs seem to fly through the jungle trees.

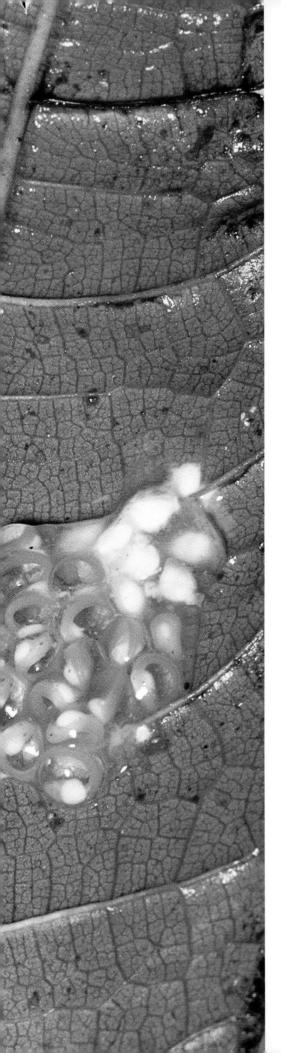

Latin America's glass frog (left) is almost as clear as its eggs. When the eggs near tadpole stage, they "drip" from the tip of the leaf into a stream (below).

"Backpacking" them in a protective pouch, a marsupial frog (below) carries its eggs until they grow into tadpoles.

Actually, they glide from high branches down to lower ones in search of insects to eat (see pages 34-35).

Even some frogs that spend most of their lives on the ground climb up on branches. Among the most unusual is one of the arrow-poison frogs. It lays its eggs under wet leaves on the jungle floor. Then one of the parents stands guard until the eggs hatch into tiny tadpoles. Now the work really begins. First, the tadpoles wiggle onto the adult frog's back. Then the parent frog climbs up the tree. Once it reaches the top, the frog goes from limb to limb, looking for tank bromeliads or other plants filled with water (see pages 24-25). Slowly the frog backs into the first tank it finds. If that tank already has a tadpole, the frog crawls out and goes off to find an empty one. The frog leaves one tadpole in each empty tank

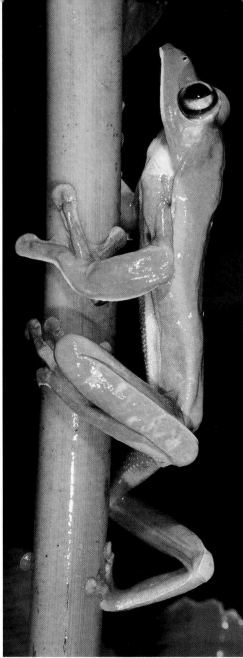

Round pads on their toes give golden-eyed leaf frogs (left) all the grip they need to climb thin stems and leap between wobbly leaves.

The arrow-poison frog (below) lives on the ground, but climbs trees to leave its tadpoles in pools of water in the centers of bromeliad plants.

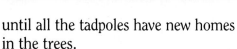

until all the tadpoles have new homes in the trees.

If the parent carrying the tadpoles is a female, she takes even more care of her youngsters. After dropping them into the water-filled tanks, she goes back to the ground to feed. Later, she makes her way back up the tree to where she left the tadpoles. This time she lays infertile eggs, ones that will not hatch. These eggs give the tadpoles extra food.

Once the tadpoles develop into froglets—almost-grown frogs—they climb down to the ground. They stay there until it's their turn to carry tadpoles to the treetops.

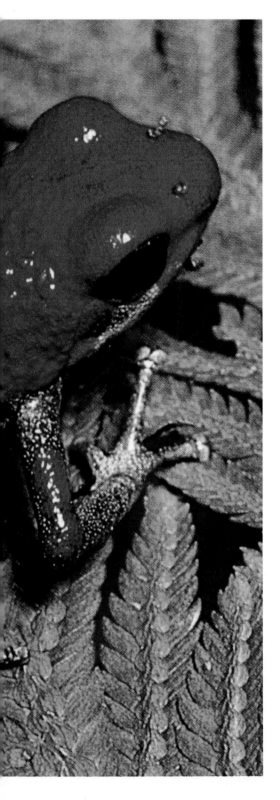

POISON ARROWS

All frogs produce poison on their skin. A lot of it is so mild that the effects can hardly be felt. But the jungles' *arrow-poison frogs* make some of the strongest natural poisons in the world. And some South American Indians use these poisons when they hunt. First, the Indians kill the frogs and heat them until the poison oozes out in shiny drops. Then they smear the drops onto the tips of their arrows and darts. The poison paralyzes monkeys and other prey but doesn't make their meat poisonous.

These arrow-poison frogs are some of the most colorful frogs in the jungle. Flame red, bright blue, black and orange—their colors are easy to spot. By advertising that they are deadly, the frogs keep enemies away.

HANGING IN THERE

The Latin American palm viper (below) kills birds and other prey with poison ten times as strong as that of some rattlesnakes.

Many visitors to the jungles expect to see trees draped with slithering, poisonous snakes. The truth is, jungle snakes—like snakes everywhere—are often hard to find. And few are poisonous.

A tree snake could be right in front of you and still not be seen. The snake's color and thin shape often make it look like the branches it hides on. To make this disguise even better, some tree snakes also sway gently back and forth as they hang from limbs. This motion helps them look like limbs blowing in the breeze.

These disguises help snakes get food. The snakes wait, unnoticed, in places where lizards and other small creatures often travel. Then they grab their prey as it passes by. Disguises also help the snakes hide from hungry eagles and other animals that hunt and eat snakes.

The blunt-headed tree snake of Costa Rica (above) can stretch its body long distances between branches in its search for lizards.

The snail-eating snake (left), also found in Costa Rican jungles, is just one of several kinds of snakes that can eat only soft prey like slugs and the bodies of snails.

47

The emerald tree boa (left), one of the most brightly colored of all South American snakes, coils around thick branches as it waits to catch birds and lizards.

Like the spider monkeys and tamanduas, some tree snakes have prehensile tails (see pages 18-19). Snakes may look like they are *all* tail, but they are mostly body. Snakes with prehensile tails can grab hold of a branch with their tails and stretch out for almost their entire length when they strike.

Tree pythons in Asia and tree boas in Latin America are able to capture many kinds of prey, including birds, monkeys, lizards—almost anything the snakes find in the trees. Both snakes catch their prey in much the same way. First they strike with open, strong jaws. Then they quickly coil around the creatures and squeeze the breath out of them. When the animals quit struggling, the snakes swallow them whole.

Some tree snakes are specialists and eat only a few kinds of food. Snail-eating snakes are built for eating snails and slugs. Their weak teeth can handle only soft prey—and slugs are certainly soft. Also, their jaws cannot open extra wide to swallow large prey the way the jaws of boas and some other snakes do. So they can swallow only small creatures. But they do this very well. A snake strikes a snail close to the shell and starts chewing. It takes the snake only about a minute to pull the snail out.

Africa's egg-eating snake lives only on eggs—and swallows them whole, shell and all. Sharp spines in the snake's throat saw open the egg. Then the snake digests the liquid and spits out the broken shell.

The green colors of these Asian snakes help them hide among the leaves of the jungle trees. The vine snake (top) hunts by day. The turquoise snake (above) hunts by night. Small pits near its nose detect the warmth of its prey in the dark.

JEEPERS! CREEPERS!

Spiders, leeches, ants, termites—the jungle floor is alive with tiny creeping and crawling creatures. You might think that animals so small couldn't be very important to the life of the jungle. But together they really add up. In the Amazon jungle, if you could collect just the tiny creatures living in the soil, they would weigh nearly four times as much as all the jaguars, sloths, and other large animals there.

Leaf-cutter ants are the gardeners of the jungle floor. First, worker ants from a leaf-cutter colony spread out through the jungle. They climb to the treetops where they cut up the leaves. Then they carry the pieces back to their underground nests. There the ants chew the leaves into small pieces and pile them in special rooms. The leaves serve as food—not for the ants, but for fungus that grows on the leaves. The ants eat the fungus.

Army ants are probably the best-known of all the tiny creatures on the jungle floor. When large groups of these ants get moving, they can be very destructive. More than twenty million army ants—nearly one for every man, woman, and child in California—may go on a march together. And they eat other small creatures that don't get out of the way. Masses of Africa's driver ants—one type of army ant—have been known to kill and strip wild pigs down to bare bones.

When on a raid, masses of army ants move out in large columns. A column may stretch the length of a

Like a pack of hungry wolves, Brazilian army ants (right) cut up a katydid to carry back to their nest. The ants travel from the jungle floor to the treetops in search of prey.

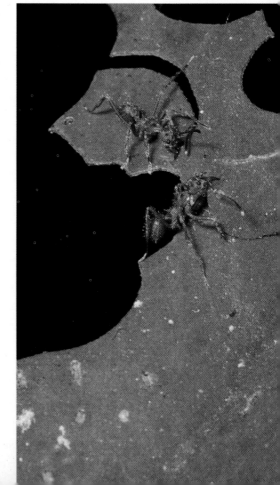

football field. The ants don't move very fast—only about a foot per minute. That works out to less than a mile per week. Fast-moving animals have no trouble getting out of the way. But sick creatures, or those that are are surrounded, soon become meals for the ants.

Small streams are no obstacle for these ants when they are on the move. The first ants to reach a stream hook their legs together and make a living bridge. The rest of the column then marches across.

Some jungle people welcome the ants' raids. Once the ants have passed through, the people return to find

Leaf-cutter ants trim leaves into small pieces (left), then carry them back to the jungle floor (above). The ants chew the leaves to make a soft, wet "garden" where they grow fungus to eat.

53

their homes free of roaches, fleas, and other insects.

After about two weeks, the column of ants stops moving. The ants must wait so their larvae can spin cocoons. While the larvae are changing into adult ants, the ant queen lays her eggs. She lays up to 300,000 in just a few days. After another week or so, the eggs hatch into larvae. At the same time, the new adult ants break out of their cocoons. With thousands of hungry larvae to feed, the colony of army ants once again starts its march to find food.

Because it is so humid, the jungle floor makes a good home for some creatures that you would expect to find in water. The best-known are the parasitic worms known as *leeches*. Most leeches are water dwellers. But some jungles also have land leeches. They ambush animals—and people—moving through the jungles. They detect heat from the warm-blooded bodies and attach themselves as the animals walk by.

Once attached, leeches feed by sucking blood from their hosts. Leeches don't feed very often, but when they do, they may take in up to ten times their weight in blood. That's enough to hold them for several months. Like vampire bats, leeches have chemicals in their saliva that keep the host's blood flowing freely, even after they finish feeding and drop off.

The Costa Rican red-kneed tarantula (above) guards its eggs in a silk cocoon. Hundreds of eggs will hatch, but only about ten of the young spiders will survive to become adults.

An Australian land leech sits on a fallen leaf (right), waiting to latch onto a passing animal and feed on its blood. Some leeches eat enough at one time to last them a year.

People in jungles find it almost impossible to avoid leeches. These tiny creatures can ease their way through the eyelets of boots and right on through a person's socks.

Spiders of all sizes also make their homes on—or under—the jungle floor. Trapdoor spiders dig holes up to a foot deep and cover them with snug-fitting, hinged doors. The spiders hide in the holes, then pop out to catch passing insects.

In Latin American jungles, some giant tarantulas live under rocks and leaves. They wait there to attack small reptiles, mammals, and insects. Some of them also spend part of the time in the trees. One of these tarantulas is the largest spider in the world. It is called the bird-eating spider, and it really does hunt birds for food.

Termites probably outnumber all other insects in the jungle. Their nests are often easy to spot. Some tower like four-foot-high mushrooms on the jungle floor. Others hang like giant clumps of dirt on the trunks of trees. But the termites themselves stay out of sight. They are busy munching away on the insides of dead trees and rotting logs.

Termites are good at chewing up this dead wood. But they can't digest it—at least not by themselves. The termites must rely on microscopic organisms called *bacteria* and *protozoa* that live in their digestive tracts. These organisms turn wood into food the termites can digest.

Termites are real pests when they chew up the wood in our homes. But in jungles, they are important recyclers. By chewing up old wood, they help turn dead trees into food for animals. Without termites, ants, beetles—and many other tiny creatures—the jungle would soon smother in its own litter.

THE RECYCLERS

Termites, worms, and other tiny creatures are recyclers. They help turn fallen leaves and other dead matter into soil or food for plants. But some of the most important recyclers are plants called *fungi*. Fungi usually grow in the form of threads spreading through the soil and litter. The threads give off chemicals that break down dead plants into minerals that trees can use. At times, the fungi poke up through the soil as mushrooms and toadstools, like the lacy stinkhorn below.

STINKY AND KILLER

S tinky" and "Killer" sound like good nicknames for gangsters. They also would make good nicknames for two of Southeast Asia's strangest jungle plants. "Stinky" is rafflesia, the largest flower in the world. Its bloom smells like hamburger left out in the sun to rot. "Killer" is the pitcher plant. It traps and kills insects for food.

Like many plants, the three-foot-wide rafflesia needs animals to help it survive. Thousands of flies gather on the flower, attracted by its strong smell. As they crawl around, they pick up pollen on their bodies. When they travel to other rafflesias, some pollen falls off and fertilizes the plants. The seeds that develop are sticky. When animals nibble on the plants, some of the seeds stick to their legs and feet. Later, these seeds fall off. If they land in the right spot, they start to grow.

For a rafflesia, the right spot to grow is inside the stem of a liana. First, the rafflesia seed sends out thin threads inside the liana to soak up water and nutrients. The threads spread this way for nearly a year and a half. Finally a bud develops and breaks through the vine's bark. It looks like a tiny head of cabbage. This bud gets larger and larger, like a rosebud that expands but doesn't open. Nine months later, the bud finally opens, spreading out its leathery orange-and-brown petals.

After taking more than two years to grow, the rafflesia blooms and fades in less than a week. But in

Rafflesias look like brown cabbages when they grow their first leathery petals (left top). They soon open into smelly flowers that are nearly a yard wide (left bottom).

The strong odor of an Asian pitcher plant (below) attracts insects. Some insects that land on the plant slip and fall into its pitcher, where a special liquid digests them.

those few days it provides the largest—and probably the smelliest—flower in the entire plant world.

While "Stinky" rafflesia needs flies or other insects to spread its pollen and seeds, "Killer" pitcher plant needs them for its dinner. The pitcher plant is said to be *carnivorous* (car-NIV-uh-russ), or meat-eating. Its prey ranges from ants and flies to cockroaches and centipedes.

Of course, pitcher plants can't pull up their roots and run around chasing their prey. So how do they get dinner? They trap it.

Pitcher plants look like colorful pitchers filled with a clear liquid. Some kinds have sweet-smelling nectar that attracts insects. Once insects land on a plant, they often crawl around looking for more nectar. Some will slide on the pitcher's slippery rim and fall into the liquid and drown. Others get the plant's wax stuck on their feet, lose their foothold, and then fall into the pitcher.

Many pitchers have chemicals in their liquid to digest the insects. Flies may be digested in two days, smaller creatures in just a few hours. The liquid isn't strong enough to hurt people, though. One 19th century explorer found the pitcher's liquid good to drink. A more recent writer noted that the liquid tastes "good, though warm."

These so-called "killer plants" tend to live in places where the soil is poor. They need the bodies of animals to give them the nutrients they must have to survive and grow.

FEW AND FAR BETWEEN

The muntjac (below), barely two feet high, barks like a dog when alarmed by leopards, tigers, or other predators. These deer are native to the jungles and mountains of southern Asia, where they live on leaves, bark, and fruit.

Scientists and explorers have discovered an interesting fact about the jungle floor: Not very many large mammals live there. Africa's grassy hills and plains are home to herds of hundreds of buffalo and thousands of wildebeest and antelope. But not the floors of Africa's jungles. Like jungles everywhere, they have fewer kinds of large mammals than you might expect. Why? Because there's not enough food for them. So little sunlight reaches the jungle floor that not enough plants grow there to support large populations of plant-eating mammals. And without a lot of plant-eaters to prey on, large meat-eating mammals don't have enough to eat, either.

Browsing animals, like the muntjac (MUNT-jack), an Asian deer, stay where they can reach low-growing leaves. Muntjacs bark to tell each other that a predator is sneaking up on them. They may keep up the noise for an hour or more.

Forest elephants browse by using their long trunks to tear down whole branches, leaves and all. Their strong stomachs take nourishment from even the toughest parts of plants.

Forest buffalo in Africa are among the jungles' few grazing animals. They are related to the African buffalo that live on the grassy plains. Where food is plentiful, African buffalo may weigh nearly a ton. But the forest buffalo grow to only half that size.

Bongos are relatives of the buffalo. They live in the thickest parts of the African jungles. Some people say these creatures chew burned wood and dirt to get salt. They must be good at finding leaves and roots to nibble on, for some weigh more than 400 pounds. When bongos are scared, they can run at full speed right through dense tangles of vines.

Elsewhere in the African jungles, large baboons called mandrills wander about turning over rocks and sticks. They are looking for fallen fruit and nuts and for small animals to eat.

More jungle animals can be seen around rivers and streams, where they go to drink, than in the forests. Peccaries, a kind of wild pig that lives from Texas to Brazil, are often near

Africa's bongo (left) and bush pig (below) eat roots and other parts of plants. The bongo feeds by day, and the bush pig feeds by night, adding reptiles and eggs to its diet.

water. So are several different rodents. Capybaras, the largest rodents in the world (see pages 80-81), often make their homes along the jungle rivers of South America. Both capybaras and the smaller, cat-sized agoutis (uh-GOO-teez) prefer to hunt during the day. But if people are around, these animals wait until sunset to come out to eat.

Tapirs also live near water. These 600-pound plant-eaters may be the oddest-looking mammals in the jungles of Asia and South America. One scientist said the long-snouted creatures looked like a "strange mixture of pig, cow, and elephant."

Where plant-eaters go, meat-eaters are sure to follow. In South America, packs of bush dogs wander near streams to hunt capybaras and other rodents. Sometimes they dive into the water and swim after their prey.

59

Heavy-looking armor of bony plates protects the forest armadillo (below) from enemies. The tapir's pear-shaped body (bottom) helps it push through patches of thick forest underbrush.

Most colorful of all mammals, a mandrill turns even brighter when it gets angry or excited (right).

Civets are catlike hunters that live in Africa and Asia. When it comes time to eat, they look for almost everything from small mammals and birds to fruit, eggs, and snakes. When some civets call each other, they sound like owls hooting. Others seem to be growling, coughing, screaming, and even laughing.

Several kinds of cats live and hunt in jungles. Their story is told on pages 64-67.

Some jungle animals have unusual defenses to protect themselves from these dangerous predators. The best-known are the armadillos and pangolins. Like living tanks, they have built-in armor.

Though many armadillos live on Latin America's plains and grasslands, some kinds also live in the jungles. All these animals are partly covered by a tough layer of horn and bone that acts as a natural shield. When threatened, the jungle armadillos pull in their feet and lie flat with only their thick armor showing.

Pangolins are covered with thick scales that make them look like walking pine cones. When threatened, they can curl up even tighter than most armadillos.

Are there more animal wonders like these hidden deep in the jungle? Probably. Scientists didn't discover the horse-sized African okapi until the early part of this century. And in South America, a kind of peccary thought to be long extinct was rediscovered by scientists exploring the jungles of Paraguay in 1972.

GENTLE GIANTS

Early African explorers said that these animals were "ferocious" and "offensive." One man reported that they would crush gun barrels with their teeth. Scientists now say that they are shy and gentle and won't even harm mice in the wild. What are these jungle terrors that have turned out to be more like gentle giants? They are the original models for King Kong: gorillas.

Gorillas will attack—but only if they are wounded or threatened. And a gorilla attack is really impressive. The animal starts by calling out—first softly and slowly, then louder and louder and faster and faster. It tears off branches and brush and throws them into the air. Then it slaps its hands on its chest or even against a tree trunk. Finally it runs toward whatever is threatening it, swatting down any plants or animals that are in the way. Then it stops with a loud SLAP! as it pounds the ground with its hand.

By this time, most other animals—and people—would be long gone. But one scientist found that he could turn off an attack before it began. He shook his head. That told the gorilla, "I mean no harm."

Most gorillas are *lowland gorillas.* They live in Africa's low-lying rain forests. But a few hundred *mountain gorillas* survive in and around national parks in the cloud forests of Zaire and Rwanda, countries in central Africa.

Mountain gorillas are endangered animals. That means they are in danger of dying out completely. They are disappearing for many reasons. Some are taken by poachers, who sneak into the parks and kill the animals. Others outside the parks die because they have no place to live. Their lands are being cleared for agriculture.

When they aren't threatened, gorillas live simple, quiet lives. They stay in groups that act as big families: an adult male leader, sometimes a few other males, several females, and a lot of youngsters.

After a morning of browsing on leafy shrubs, the adults settle down for a nap while the youngsters play. The small gorillas swing on vines, toss and tumble on the ground, and even play follow-the-leader.

The next day brings more of the same. As one scientist wrote, "The gorilla's life consists of sleeping and feeding and sleeping some more."

A devoted mother, the female mountain gorilla (left) rarely leaves her youngster's side. Males, like this lowland gorilla (below left), may also take time to play with their offspring.

King Kong

King Kong, a make-believe giant gorilla in the movies, acted like a human by falling in love with a woman. Real gorillas wouldn't behave like King Kong, but sometimes they do things that humans do. Gorillas lie on their backs with their arms under their heads—just like people on a warm day in the park. And like some human children, gorilla youngsters have tantrums when they don't get their own way.

PAWS, CLAWS, AND JAWS

Cats are the jungles' top predators. That means that they live by hunting and eating other animals, but almost no other animals live by hunting and eating them.

Many of these cats belong to a group that scientists call the small cats. Some small cats, like the marbled cats and leopard cats of Asia, are about the size of large house cats. Others, like the ocelot of South America, are as large as cocker spaniels. The largest of the small cat group, the cougars, grow to be as heavy as St. Bernards.

Small size doesn't keep even the smallest cats from being dangerous. When it goes hunting, a leopard cat can bring down a young deer. Unlike some of the cats, leopard cats are not scared away when people move into the jungle. They often stay nearby and raid the settlers' farms and villages to catch chickens.

Fishing cats, as their name suggests, like to catch their meals in rivers and streams. These Asian animals crouch along the banks and scoop out fish with their sharp claws. Like most wild cats, they don't seem to mind getting wet. They will often wade or swim as they go from place to place.

Some scientists put Asia's clouded leopard in a class all by itself. Like a leopard, this cat has spots. But its spots are much larger than a leopard's and look a bit like fleecy "clouds." Clouded leopards are so hard to find that not much is known about the way they live. Some reports

say that they hunt in trees at twilight, catching monkeys and birds. Other reports say that the animals may also hunt on the ground during the day.

Not many people have heard of some of the small cats. But almost everyone knows the jungles' large cats: jaguars, leopards, and tigers.

In Latin America, people used to worship jaguars. Mayans in Mexico and Central America built altars for

The tastiest dish to an ocelot (far left) is an agouti, a mammal the size of a spaniel. The fishing cat (above) scoops up fish with webbed paws. The jaguarundi (left) eats birds, frogs, and mammals—even figs!

The black panther (below) is really a leopard. In the high mountains and thick forests of Asia, almost half of the leopards are black panthers.

Tigers (right) are the largest of the big cats, weighing up to 800 pounds. Yet their black, white, and golden coats can make them nearly invisible in shadows and tall grass.

chokes it or bites it to death. Leopards often store their food in trees so they can eat later. They are so strong they can climb while dragging along animals heavier than they are.

According to an old saying, leopards can't change their spots. But not all leopards have spots that are easy to see. Black panthers, common in African and Asian jungles, are really leopards with dark hair and nearly hidden spots.

Asia's tigers are the largest of the large cats and deserve the title "King of the Jungle." Some people give that title to lions, but lions really prefer living on grassy plains and in open woodlands—not in jungles!

A loud "Boo!" may scare away a jaguar, but tigers don't seem to be afraid of anything. They will even attack dangerous wild boars, pig-like animals that can fight back with large, sharp tusks.

Tigers are strong, too. One time some people found an animal that a tiger had killed and dragged away to hide. When they tried to move the dead animal, more than a dozen men pulling together couldn't budge it.

In parts of the world, the future of wild cats is threatened. Their home ranges are disappearing as people clear the jungles. Some cats, like the small leopard cats, survive by preying on domestic animals the people bring with them—particularly chickens. But other cats, like Asia's marbled cats and golden cats, can't adjust to people. They are becoming more and more rare.

these cats and named the jaguar "king of the underworld."

When hunting, jaguars travel by themselves. They cover up to twenty square miles as they search for large and medium-sized plant eaters. Some jaguars attack and eat crocodiles. Like many animals, they prefer to leave people alone. One scientist counted on this when he spotted a jaguar close to his tent. He shouted "Boo!"—and the animal ran away.

Leopards, which live in Asia and Africa, stalk their prey at night. They quietly follow large and small animals. With a quick jump, a leopard catches its prey by the throat and either

HOP, SLITHER, AND SCURRY

The wide mouth of this South American horned frog (left) hides teeth sharp enough to kill lizards, mice, and other horned frogs.

Looking like a tiny dinosaur, a basilisk lizard (above) escapes predators by running on water. Its speed—and large hind feet—help keep it afloat.

Golden toads (left) are as hard to find as gold nuggets. So far, they have been spotted only in a Costa Rican cloud forest. These are male frogs. The females are dark green or black with red spots or even the color of cream.

Some of them are cannibals. Some of them swallow creatures even larger than themselves. And one of them walks on water. What are they? They are the frogs, snakes, and lizards of the jungle floor.

People usually think of frogs as shy little creatures, hopping out of sight at the slightest sound. And many frogs behave just that way. But not the horned frogs of South America. These three-inch-high animals are little terrors. They have teeth and snap at almost anything that comes near them—including other horned frogs. There aren't many of these frogs in the jungles. One scientist thinks this is because so many are eaten by their relatives.

Latin America's golden toads push and shove each other around, too, but only during mating time. When the rainy season begins, golden toads gather in pools of water to find mates. Then it's a big free-for-all as the male frogs kick and push each other for chances to mate with females. It's all over in less than a week. The eggs have been laid and

Africa's Gaboon viper (above) delivers its poison through fangs up to two inches long, the longest fangs of any snake. But this viper often will not bite, even when it is picked up.

fertilized and the adult frogs have left to find food.

Frogs and other creatures have dangerous company on the jungle floor. Some of the most deadly are the snakes. Many of the largest snakes in the world live in the jungles. Some measure more than 25 feet long. One of the largest of these is the anaconda, a type of boa that lives in the rivers of South America.

Pythons are African and Asian relatives of the boas. Some grow almost as long as their South American cousins and can capture pigs and small deer. Like tree-dwelling boas and pythons, these snakes strike

quickly. Then they wrap themselves around their prey and squeeze until the animal can't breathe.

Boas and pythons have flexible jaws that spread wide apart as they swallow. It's not unusual to see a python or boa with a whole pig or small deer in its stomach. The meal is much bigger around than the snake's mouth! The snakes may take weeks to digest these creatures, bones and all.

King cobras and bushmasters are probably the jungles' best-known poisonous snakes. These two are the longest poisonous snakes in the world. Few sights are as awesome as

70

Asia's king cobras are the world's longest poisonous snakes. This young one (left) may grow to be as long as a car. A bushmaster (below), which can grow to 12 feet, is the longest poisonous snake in the New World.

a 15-foot-long king cobra ready to strike. This Asian reptile raises its head four feet or so off the ground, spreading its wide hood and hissing.

The 12-foot-long Latin American bushmaster hunts at night, using tiny heat sensors on its head to find prey. The snake can feel the warmth of a mouse from six inches away.

The Gaboon viper of Africa is half the length of a bushmaster, but it is often heavier. This poisonous snake's colorful markings make it stand out when seen in bright light. But in the shade of the jungle, they serve as a disguise to help it disappear among the fallen leaves.

Lizards make ideal meals for these snakes—but not because they taste good. Lizards are just the right shape, long and usually thin, for snakes to swallow easily. In some places, snakes are lizards' chief enemies.

Some lizards fight back with spiny tails. Some have tails that break away when enemies grab them. Some stand so still they look like sticks of wood. Basilisk lizards run away, and when they do, not even streams or deep puddles stop them. These Latin American creatures raise up on their hind legs and keep on going. Their wide feet and fringed toes help them scamper across the water's surface.

BIRDS OF A DIFFERENT FEATHER

Not all jungle birds stay in the treetops. Some wander about on the forest floor. Why are they down there? Often because they can't fly very well. Or, like the nearly wingless cassowaries, because they can't fly at all. Some birds that *can* fly well also live on the ground, but for other reasons. Africa's Guinea fowl gather there to find food. And the male bowerbirds of New Guinea and Australia go there in breeding season to build their special displays that will attract mates.

In New Guinea, many people have seen the cassowary's tracks. And they have heard its grunts and snorts, squeaks and howls. But few people have seen these birds in the wild. Cassowaries stay deep in the jungle, traveling alone as they search for fruit that has fallen from the trees.

People are probably just as happy not to come across cassowaries in the jungle, for the birds can be dangerous. Some cassowaries grow as tall as people, and their long, sharp toes make deadly weapons. Trapped birds kick out and cut any animals trying to attack them.

The most striking feature of the cassowary is its head. It is topped by a hard, bony helmet called a *casque* (CASK). That is the same name given to the big tube on hornbills' beaks (see page 30). The cassowary's casque may protect the bird's head as it dashes at thirty miles per hour through dense underbrush. But recently someone watched a cassowary in a zoo push dirt around with its

Smaller than a chicken, the crested Guinea fowl (left) finds safety in flocks of up to 30 birds. The man-sized cassowary (below) lives alone until mating season. After mating, the male birds incubate the eggs and stay with the youngsters for their first year of life.

casque to find food. Maybe wild birds in the jungle dig through the leaves this way to find fallen fruit.

Some African Guinea fowl have bony helmets like those of the cassowary. Scientists don't know what these helmets are used for, though. Other Guinea fowl have feathery crests. The crested Guinea fowl, for example, has tufts of curly, black feathers on top of its head. Though these birds are strong fliers, they hunt and peck on the ground for seeds, roots, insects, and even small frogs. Flocks of up to thirty of these birds often venture outside the jungle as they feed.

In New Guinea and Australia, bowerbirds are the architects of the jungle floor. During courtship, the male birds use sticks, moss, and flowers to build displays called *bowers.* In peoples' gardens, a bower is a quiet place enclosed by a vine-covered frame. Some bowerbirds build enclosures a lot like that. The birds' bowers are designed to catch the attention of passing females.

The most colorful male bowerbirds build the simplest bowers. Some of their bowers are just cleared areas of jungle floor dotted with leaves. The birds' bright colors are enough to attract females for mating.

Other male bowerbirds may build thatched huts and towers up to six feet high. That's a big job for these birds that are no larger than crows. The males may also add bright leaves and colorful objects they find lying around in the jungle.

Once the birds mate, the bower's job is over. The male leaves and the female goes somewhere else to build her nest, lay eggs, and raise the young by herself.

Busy building with twigs (above), a male golden bowerbird attempts to attract mates to his courting area. Some bowerbirds make their bowers bigger by adding to what they built the year before.

STRANGEST BIRD
IN THE WORLD

A hoatzin chick (right) uses both its beak and tiny claws on the "elbows" of its wings to pull itself up from one limb to the next.

Beside the jungle rivers of South America live some birds that scientists have called "the strangest birds in the world." These are the hoatzins (ho-WATT-sins). They have red eyes and gold-colored feathers. They live in flimsy nests hanging low over rivers and streams. And they are about the size of crows. But hoatzins have little in common with crows—or with any other birds.

Hoatzins are different from other birds from the moment they hatch. The young birds start out with tiny claws on their wings. Few other birds are built this way. The young hoatzins can't fly until they are about two months old. Until then, they use the claws to help them climb from branch to branch.

By the time they are ready to fly, the young hoatzins start to lose their claws. But these birds still don't behave the way most other birds do. When they are a year old, and their parents have new eggs in the nest, they stick around to help take care of the family. The year-old birds sometimes even sit on their parents' eggs until they hatch.

When monkeys or other animals come by and try to steal the eggs, the entire hoatzin family gets into the act. The adults and older offspring

The hoatzins' strange appearance is matched by their odd behavior, which includes eating leaves and babysitting.

screech to drive away the invaders. They also spread their wings to make themselves look large and dangerous.

At the same time, the youngest hoatzins jump into the water beneath their nest and swim away to safety. Usually this escape route works. But sometimes the youngsters drop down near a hungry caiman—related to the crocodile—or into a school of piranhas. They end up as another animal's meal after all.

When the hoatzins eat, they still do things in their own unusual way. They eat leaves, something few other birds in the world do. And they grind up the food in their crops, special pouches just above their stomachs. *No* other birds do that. Other birds use their crops to store food before grinding it up in their gizzards.

To do all the grinding that tough leaves require, hoatzins have a crop that is larger than usual. This oversized crop leaves room for only a small keel, or breastbone, where their wing muscles are attached. That means the birds' wing muscles have to be small, too. And with only small muscles to power their wings, the hoatzins can fly only short distances without tiring out. When a hoatzin lands, it plops down and rests on its backside like a tired-out runner.

WET AND WILD

The South American pirarucu (below), one of the world's largest freshwater fish, easily outweighs the young boy hauling it to shore.

Some of the world's greatest rivers flow through the jungles. The Amazon in South America is the largest river anywhere. It carries eleven times as much water as the Mississippi, the largest river in the United States. From the Amazon to the Zaire River in Africa and the Mekong in Southeast Asia, jungle rivers support a tremendous variety of fish and other wildlife.

The Amazon alone has more than 1,000 kinds of catfish. Some are barely an inch long. Others are larger and heavier than a grown man. In Asia, a single Mekong River giant catfish—weighing in at 600 pounds—can feed an entire village.

Many people have heard tales of piranhas, the meat-eating fish of South America. Schools of piranhas can strip the flesh from animals in just a few minutes. Their teeth are so sharp that natives use them to cut hair and sharpen weapons.

Piranhas aren't the only jungle fish with strong teeth. Several kinds of South American fish eat seeds as hard as almonds or English walnuts. Some of these fish swallow the seeds whole. Others crush them with one powerful bite.

Fish breathe with gills, taking in oxygen that is dissolved in the water. When the dry season comes and water levels fall, many jungle fish retreat to deeper water. If they are stranded and left without water, they die. But lungfish have lungs and breathe air at the water's surface. They have no problem when their streams dry up.

They bury themselves in the mud. Then they breathe through cracks in the dirt and wait until the rainy season returns.

Getting oxygen sometimes gets the giant pirarucu fish of South America into trouble. These six-foot-long air breathers have to surface every 15 minutes or so. When they do, native fishermen try to catch them with harpoons or bows and arrows.

Giant reptiles also make their homes in jungle rivers. South America's anacondas are among the longest snakes in the world, measuring more than 25 feet long. That's as long as a big station wagon. They prowl the riverbanks in search of mammals and other creatures to eat. Sometimes they even attack large crocodilelike caimans (KAY-mans).

Caimans and crocodiles rarely hunt animals on the land. They float just

The bearded catfish (top), which looks more like a scrub brush than a fish, was discovered in Venezuela in 1985. The African lungfish (above) lives in swamps that often dry up. It survives by breathing with its lungs when exposed to air. It burrows deep in the mud until it rains.

South America's matamata turtle (left), whose jaws are too weak to chew big bites, sucks in mouthfuls of water to capture small creatures. Its neighbor the anaconda snake is strong enough to overpower a caiman (below).

under the surface, with only their eyes poking up above the water. Patiently, they wait for animals to come to the river for a drink—and then they attack.

Scientists have described how some caimans leave the river to lay their eggs next to termite nests. The termites add to their nests until they surround the eggs. The nests keep half of the eggs warm and half of them cool. The warm eggs develop into male caimans. The cool ones develop into females. When the baby caimans hatch, they break out of the nests and head back for the river.

Another river reptile, the matamata (MAH-tuh-muh-TAH), has been called the strangest turtle in the world. It has an extra-long neck with flaps of skin hanging down and a lumpy shell. It looks more like a piece of moss-covered wood than a turtle. Its mouth is farther back on its head than its tiny eyes. And its flat head is dotted with loose flaps of skin. Unlike most turtles, the matamata has weak jaws. It cannot snap up prey the way other turtles do. Instead, it opens its jaws wide whenever a small fish or tadpole swims by. Water rushing into the turtle's mouth brings the creature's dinner with it.

Mammals are important jungle river creatures, too. In fact, the heaviest animals in the Amazon jungle are river mammals. They are manatees, known locally as "cow fish." These animals sometimes grow to weigh more than a thousand pounds on their diet of water plants—100 pounds a day!

Manatees are coming to the rescue of a jungle lake in Brazil. The lake formed behind a dam and was soon overrun with water plants. As the plants rotted, the water became acidic and started wearing out the dam's power-generating equipment. Now scientists have brought in manatees to eat the plants. The scientists hope the animals can keep the lake clear *and* protect the generating equipment.

Scientists also hope that the manatees will raise families in the lakes. Like Florida manatees, Amazon manatees are threatened with extinction. In recent years, they have increased in number, but their future is still in doubt.

The giant river otters of South America are also heavy eaters. Just one pair of six-foot-long otters may eat three tons of fish in a year. People who have watched these creatures describe them as playful and unafraid. Early explorers wrote that otters by the dozen would surround their canoes, barking like curious dogs.

Amazon dolphins, another South American river mammal, are also playful at times. When the river rises, these freshwater dolphins can be seen swimming among the flooded trees. Gray dolphins and pink dolphins twist and turn as they chase fish for their dinner. Sometimes the gray dolphins stand on their tails like the dolphins in an aquarium. Why? This is just one more jungle mystery to be solved.

GIANTS AND MIDGETS

The mouse opossum (below) is a scrappy fighter, ready to make a meal of this giant grasshopper. The mouse deer (bottom) is a shy plant eater, and runs from other animals.

Some of the animals and plants that live in jungles are real record-setters. Some are larger than any of their relatives living outside the jungles. And others are the very smallest of their kind.

The world's largest owls and eagles live in the tropics and prey on jungle animals from the treetops down to the ground. The largest bats, members of a group called *flying foxes,* live in the jungles of Southeast Asia. The largest flowers live nearby. These are the rafflesias, found on Borneo, Sumatra, and other islands of Southeast Asia (see pages 56-57).

Other record-setters include the largest wild pig—the 600-pound forest hog of Africa—and the largest armadillo—the giant armadillo of South America. Some capybaras, the largest rodents, live in the jungles as well as on grasslands in Latin America. They live anywhere they can find enough water.

Jungle insects, reptiles, and amphibians set records for size, too. At more than seven inches long, South America's Hercules beetle is probably the world's largest beetle. South America is also home to some of the longest snakes, the anacondas. Adult anacondas are more than 25 feet long, longer than the average living room. In Africa, the first goliath frog ever caught set a world's record for frogs: nearly ten inches long. According to scientists who were there, an even larger one got away.

The prettiest jungle giants are probably the birdwing butterflies of

Queen Alexandra's birdwing (left above) is now protected in a New Guinea reserve. The capybara (left below) can be found in jungles and grasslands from Panama to Argentina.

Southeast Asia. Some have wings that spread nearly a foot across. Collectors prize these butterflies both for their size and for their colors: yellows, greens, and sometimes golds.

Jungles have their share of tiny creatures, too. Africa is home to the world's smallest hippos and squirrels. It would take more than ten pygmy hippos to weigh as much as their full-sized relatives. And the pygmy squirrels really look like midget mice. South America has the tiny mouse opossum. The smallest member of the opossum family, it measures only three to seven inches long.

The world's smallest rhinos and bears live in Asian jungles. A Sumatran jungle rhino weighs about a third as much as the white rhino on the African plains. And an Asian sun bear weighs barely a fourth as much as an American black bear.

Asian jungles are also home to the eight-inch-high mouse deer. Mouse deer are the tiniest of the even-toed hoofed mammals, a very large group that includes pigs, cattle, and sheep.

Jungles also shelter the smallest mammals of all. These are the pygmy white-toothed shrew and Kitti's hog-nosed bat. Each is about the size of a large bumblebee. It would take more than a dozen of them just to weigh one ounce. The bats live in Thailand in an area that once had thick forests. Though the jungles have been cut down, some of these bats survive near tree plantations. The shrews are more widespread. They range from Asia to Europe.

PEOPLE AND THE JUNGLE

LIVING IN JUNGLES

For some people, the jungle is more than just a dark, deep forest filled with strange animals. It is home. Nearly every jungle has its native people. They live in balance with nature—hunting, fishing, and gathering plants and farming in small clearings.

Some of the best-known jungle natives are Africa's "little people," the Pygmies. Adults are barely 4½ feet tall. They build their camps deep in the rain forests of Zaire. That puts them right in the center of Africa. No one knows just how long the Pygmies have lived there. Ancient Egyptians wrote about them more than 4,000 years ago.

The Pygmies live by hunting and by gathering fruit, nuts, and berries. They use nets to capture wild hogs, antelope, and other creatures. They also hunt with knives and spears and use poisoned arrows to kill monkeys high in trees. And when honey is available, everyone joins in the search for the beehives to collect the honey to eat.

Whatever they need, the Pygmies say they can find it in the jungle. "The forest is a father and mother to us," they say. "It gets us everything we need—food, clothing, shelter, warmth . . . and affection."

When things go wrong—such as when dangerous animals raid their camps—Pygmies say that the forest is sleeping. "We wake it up by singing to it," they say. "Then everything will be well and good again."

But the Pygmies know that their future is tied to the future of the jungle. "When the Forest dies," they say, "we shall die."

Like the Pygmies, the Agta people of the Philippines depend on the jungles for almost all their needs. They hunt deer, wild pigs, monkeys, and other animals for food. They catch fish in the jungle rivers. They use the bark of the trees to make clothing, palm branches to build homes, leaves to cushion their beds, and wood to make tools. They trade jungle products with outsiders to get metal tools, cooking pots, and rice.

The Agta people are also different from Pygmies and many other jungle tribes: both women and men hunt. In many other tribes, only the men hunt animals. The women garden or gather roots and berries. Even when Pygmies go hunting, the men carry the spears and let the women and children chase

Pygmies use their skill with bows and arrows (below) to kill animals for food. Other jungle people cut palm leaves to make roofs for their huts (opposite) and grow small gardens of forest plants to eat.

game into their nets. But an Agta mother thinks nothing of taking her long knife or bow and arrow and chasing a deer for days until it collapses. Most young girls also join in the hunts, helping to cut up the meat and carry it home.

Scientists studying South America's jungles have found that long ago two kinds of tribes lived there: river people and land people. The river people are all gone now, but scientists have some ideas about how they lived. They gathered by the hundreds in large villages along the Amazon. The river provided enough fish to feed large groups year after year. Like the

The jungle is both a home and a school to Yanomamo children, who learn firsthand about fish (right), birds (far right), and other creatures. Though they do not study reading or writing, the youngsters learn how to get everything they need from the wild.

After breaking up a termite nest, Yano-mamo Indians of South America (left) gather the termites' larvae, which they eat. The larvae are said to be tasty and nutritious.

land people, river people hunted birds, monkeys, and other animals. But they also caught fish with nets, baskets, and bows and arrows. Sometimes they crushed poisonous plants and threw them into the river. The poison stunned the fish, which floated to the surface where the people easily scooped them up.

When the river flooded each year, the rising waters would bring new soil washed down from the interior. After the water level went down, the river people planted their crops.

Land people still live in the Amazon jungles. They stay in small villages of just a few dozen people each. There is not enough food—including wild pigs, monkeys, and birds—to support more. Some tribes clear small patches of forest to plant corn and cassava (which we know as tapioca). But when the nutrients in the soil are used up and crops no longer grow, the entire village moves on. The trees and vines of the jungle soon take over the cultivated land.

No one knows when these South American jungle people arrived in the Americas. But by the time European explorers got there in the 1500s, there may have been more than six million Indians living in the Amazon region. Today the number is under 250,000. Many of the jungle people were killed or died from diseases brought in by outsiders. Some were moved into the growing towns. But other people may still live in the vast Amazon jungle. When engineers in Brazil were clearing jungle lands in the 1970s to build a highway, new groups of natives were discovered every year. For all we know, other people are still there, just beyond the reach of the modern world.

GIFTS OF THE JUNGLE

The jungles are far from where most of us live. But one way or another, these forests touch our lives almost every day. If you've ever eaten a chocolate bar or sat on a teakwood chair, you've used a product that began in the jungles.

Consider just the foods and spices. Cacao trees, which give us chocolate, grow wild in the Amazon rain forests. Though most cocoa today comes from large tree farms, the trees on the farms all came from jungle ancestors. African kola nuts add flavor to many popular cola soft drinks. And the list goes on: chicle for chewing gum, cinnamon, nutmeg, and vanilla. These are just a few of the food products discovered in jungles.

Rubber, another product of tree farms, also comes from trees with jungle ancestors. The trees' inner bark contains a liquid called *latex*. When the latex is heated or treated with chemicals, tiny particles in the liquid stick together and form a solid lump of rubber.

The jungle trees themselves provide wood for many uses. Lightweight balsa from Ecuador may turn up as a toy airplane model or as scenery for a TV show. African mahogany and Asian teak are both popular for expensive furniture. And trees of many kinds may end up as paneling on the walls of a family room or as plywood under wall-to-wall carpet.

Jungle plants provide medicines, too. Quinine, for treating malaria, first came from the bark of jungle trees and shrubs. And a drug for

Sap from certain jungle trees, like the one above, is collected and heated or mixed with chemicals to make natural rubber. Seeds of the red "lipstick" tree (right) produce a yellow dye used for coloring soap, cheese, and even rubber.

The fruit of durian trees (right) is a popular treat in Southeast Asia. Durians are jungle trees, but now are grown on tree farms. The fruit tastes like a custard mixed with almonds, but it smells like rotten onions—or worse!

Chocolate comes from beans that grow in pods on the jungle cacao tree (left). Bananas (below) come from trees that first grew wild in the jungles of Africa.

treating high blood pressure was discovered in jungle roots.

Indians in the Amazon jungles use more than 1,000 different plants for their homemade cures. Tribal medicine men in many places use jungle herbs to treat a variety of ailments, including asthma and malaria. Some herbs have proved so effective that they are now sold in drugstores all around the world.

Jungles also help people by soaking up rainfall that would otherwise flood low-lying towns. Later, rivers and streams carry the water out of the forests in a steady flow. This gives farms and cities a year-round supply of water for irrigation and for drinking. As the jungles are cut down, the people downstream face periods of flooding and drought.

Jungles also absorb the strong winds of tropical storms. Scientists say that without the protection of the jungles, tropical countries suffer even greater damage when hurricanes and typhoons hit. Further, when the jungles have been cut down, the heavy rainfalls wash the soil into rivers even faster. In some countries, rivers are filling up with enough soil to create new islands.

What's in the future? Of course, no one knows for sure. But scientists worry that if all the jungles are destroyed, the world will never know many useful foods and medicines yet to be discovered. And with less protection from flood, drought, and storm, people in the tropics will face more dangers than ever before.

JUNGLES UNDER ATTACK

Can you imagine a huge jungle the size of Florida or Pennsylvania just disappearing? That's how much tropical rain forest is cleared each year. At the present rate of destruction, nine countries will lose all of their jungles within thirty years. And two dozen more countries in the tropics will lose their jungles within the next century.

Why is this happening?

In some places, the trees are cut down to use as timber. After all, wood is one of the many valuable gifts of the jungles. But this gift may turn out to be the jungles' curse as well. Unless these valuable trees are allowed to grow back, nothing will be left for people to harvest in the future. One jungle was burned to make room for planting fast-growing trees to be chopped up into 45 million chopsticks a month to send to Japan.

Some Central American jungles have been cleared to make cattle ranches. But the beef these ranches produce is not for the people of those Latin American countries. Much of it is shipped north for fast-food restaurants in the United States.

In some places, rain forests are being cleared to give the many people moving from the cities to the jungles a place to live and grow food. This is a problem because the soil in rain forests is not rich. After three or four years, harvests become poor. The farmers must clear even more land and start all over. Jungle tribes clear forests to grow food, but the tribes are small and they clear only small sections. When they move on, the jungle soon takes over the small plots they leave behind.

When modern farmers move into the jungles, they clear big areas of land. They often clear the land with bulldozers. Heavy rains soon wash away what few nutrients the soil has, and the hot sun turns the ground hard as brick.

Some jungle land disappears under the lakes of mammoth power dams. In one country, the world's fourth largest dam will flood more than 760 square miles of jungle. That's equal to flooding the cities of Atlanta, Boston, Chicago, Denver, and El Paso. The homelands of many jungle tribes lie in the area to be flooded. And plans are in the works for more than two dozen other dams to be built in the same area.

Sometimes the jungles are hurt by natural disasters. In 1982 and 1983, a forest fire on the island of Borneo burned an area the size of Delaware and Maryland combined. Reports called it "the most destructive forest fire in recorded history." Even if the fire hadn't destroyed these jungles, their future was in doubt. A half million families in need of a place to live were getting ready to move to the island and build homes.

In a few spots, the rate of destruction is slowing down. People are starting to recognize the value of jungles. But until people find other ways to meet their needs for food, lumber, electricity, and places to live, the jungles are threatened.

Some of the toughest jungle trees, like the Brazilian massanduba at left, are often cut to use in buildings. Entire sections of jungle, like that below, may be cleared for farming.

WHAT'S BEING DONE?

The loss of the world's jungles is everyone's loss. One way or another, jungles help people in every country every day. Yet every day more jungle land is destroyed. It is important for everyone to ask, "How can we save the jungles?"

First of all, people *everywhere* need to understand that the jungles are worth saving. They need to be shown how the jungles help them. Even in tropical countries, many people do not know how useful jungles really are. They think jungles are wastelands and that it doesn't hurt to cut them down. So, education is one key to the jungles' survival.

To help educate people, scientists are working to discover more about the plants and animals that live in the jungles. Some countries have set aside areas just for this purpose.

An unusual opportunity for creating a jungle study area came when the Panama Canal was built. The Canal's locks are like small dams. As the water rose behind the locks, large lakes were created. Mountaintops soon became islands. The governor of the Canal Zone set aside one of the largest islands, Barro Colorado, just for research. Today, the Smithsonian Tropical Research Institute manages the island, and scientists from all over the world study there.

Africa's Kibale Forest Project in Uganda is another center for scientific study. People working at the Project can observe leopards, golden cats, swamp antelope, red colobus monkeys, and hundreds of kinds of birds.

Many countries are also setting aside large jungle areas as parks. No houses or factories can be built in the parks, so the plants and animals living there aren't disturbed. The South American countries of Brazil, Bolivia, Peru, Ecuador, and Venezuela have already set aside enough land to cover the state of Mississippi.

Costa Rica, in Central America, is said to have one of the best park systems in the world. Parks have been set up there to protect not only the rain forests and cloud forests, but also the land around volcanoes and even the coral reefs offshore.

But parks alone are not large enough to keep all the plants and animals alive or to protect tropical countries from flood, drought, and storm damage. More must be done to protect even larger areas. One key is finding better ways to grow crops in the tropics. If they can keep the same area of land producing food year after year, farmers will not need to keep cutting down more jungle to replace worn-out land.

Some scientists also recommend growing more trees on large tree farms. These trees would be used instead of jungle trees for pulpwood, timber, and other purposes. Where possible, the tree farms should be developed on lands that already have been cleared.

There are no easy answers to the question, "How can we save the jungles?" But answers are needed soon. And with the support of all the people, a lot can be done.

INDEX

Illustrations are in **boldface** type.

Cover: (orangutan) Alain Compost/Bruce Coleman, Ltd. **Page 1:** (spatulate-nosed frog) Zig Leszczynski/Animals Animals. **2-3:** (leopard) J. Van Gruisen/Ardea London. **4-5:** (Costa Rican cloud forest) Michael Fogden/Bruce Coleman, Inc. **6:** Michael Fogden. **6-7:** Carl W. Rettenmeyer. **8-9:** (map) Pam McCoy. **9:** Karl Weidmann.

LIFE IN THE TREES

10-11: (langur monkeys) Gunter Ziesler/Bruce Coleman, Ltd. **12-13:** Donald R. Perry. **13:** Richard LaVal/Animals Animals. **14:** Left, Clifford & Dawn Frith; right, David Cavagnaro/DRK Photo. **15:** RKO Radio Pictures, Inc./ Movie Stills Archives. **16-17:** Luiz Claudio Marigo. **17:** Top, Stanley Breeden; bottom, Peter Steyn/Ardea London. **18:** Left, Luiz Claudio Marigo; right, Michael Fogden/Oxford Scientific Films. **19:** Warren Garst/Tom Stack & Associates. **20:** Erwin A. Bauer. **21:** Left, Jeffrey A. McNeely; right, Wolfgang Bayer. **22-23:** Michael Fogden. **24:** Michael Fogden/Earth Scenes. **25:** Michael Fogden. **26:** Clifford & Dawn Frith. **27:** Left, Karl Weidmann; right, Clifford & Dawn Frith. **28:** Clifford & Dawn Frith. **28-29:** Tom McHugh/National Audubon Society Collection/P.R. **29:** Michael Fogden. **30:** Karl Weidmann. **31:** Top, Brian J. Coates/Bruce Coleman, Inc.; right, A.J. Mobbs/Bruce Coleman, Ltd. **32-33:** Neil Rettig/F.R.E.E., Ltd. **34-35:**

Tom McHugh. **35:** Top, Dr. Ivan Polunin/Bruce Coleman, Inc.; bottom, Peter Ward/ Bruce Coleman, Inc. **36:** Michael Fogden. **37:** Top left, Eric Lindgren/Ardea London; top right, M.D. Tuttle/Bat Conservation International; bottom, Michael Fogden. **38:** Top, Kjell B. Sandved; bottom, Clifford & Dawn Frith. **39:** Top left, Loren McIntyre; top right, Carol Hughes/Bruce Coleman, Ltd.; bottom, Edward S. Ross. **40:** Both, Michael Fogden. **41:** All, Edward S. Ross. **42-43:** Michael Fogden. **43:** Top, Roy W. McDiarmid; bottom, Michael Fogden/Oxford Scientific Films. **44:** Richard LaVal/Animals Animals. **44-45:** Michael Fogden. **45:** Victor Englebert. **46:** Marilyn K. Krog. **47:** Both, Michael Fogden. **48:** James H. Carmichael, Jr. **49:** Both, David M. Dennis/Tom Stack & Associates.

LIFE ON THE GROUND

50-51: (leopard) Anthony Bannister. **52-53:** Top, Edward S. Ross; bottom, Michael Fogden. **53:** Michael Fogden. **54-55:** Michael Fogden. **55:** Left, Bertram G. Murray/Animals Animals; right, Michael Fogden/Oxford Scientific Films. **56:** Top, Alain Compost/Bruce Coleman, Ltd.; bottom, Kjell B. Sandved. **57:** Michael Freeman. **58:** Stanley Breeden. **59:** Left, Tom McHugh/ National Audubon Society Collection/P.R.; right, Anthony Bannister. **60:** Top,

Edward S. Ross; bottom, Luiz Claudio Marigo. **61:** Toni Angermayer/National Audubon Society Collection/P.R. **62:** John Cancalosi. **62-63:** Peter G. Veit. **63:** The Granger Collection, New York. **64:** James H. Carmichael/Bruce Coleman, Inc. **65:** Top, Belinda Wright; bottom, Fulvio Eccardi/Bruce Coleman, Inc. **66:** Phil Degginger/Bruce Coleman, Inc. **67:** Erwin & Peggy Bauer. **68-69:** Michael Fogden. **69:** Top, Hector Rivarola; right, Doug Wechsler. **70-71:** Top, Shekar Dattatri; bottom, Eric and David Hosking. **71:** Michael Fogden/Animals Animals. **72:** Top, Anthony Bannister; bottom, Clifford & Dawn Frith. **73:** Clifford & Dawn Frith. **74-75:** Stuart Strahl/NYZS. **75:** Stuart Strahl/NYZS. **76:** Loren McIntyre. **77:** Top, Robert Noonan; bottom, Zig Leszczynski/Animals Animals. **78:** R.W. Van Devender. **78-79:** Wolfgang Bayer/Bruce Coleman, Inc. **80:** Top, Carl W. Rettenmeyer; bottom, Bill & Claire Leimbach. **81:** Top, Belinda Wright; bottom, George Schaller.

PEOPLE AND THE JUNGLE

82-83: (Yanomamo Indians, South America) Victor Englebert, ©1982 Time-Life Books B.V. from The Peoples of the Wild series. **84:** Edward S. Ross. **85:** Norman Meyers/Bruce Coleman, Inc. **86-87:** All, Victor Englebert. **88:** Top, Loren McIntyre; middle, Kjell B. Sandved;

bottom, John Everingham. **89:** Top, Heather Angel; bottom, James H. Carmichael, Jr. **90-91:** Top, Loren McIntyre; bottom, Victor Englebert. **92-93:** (proboscis monkey) Alain Compost/Bruce Coleman, Ltd.

Library of Congress Cataloging-in-Publication Data

Wonders of the jungle

Includes index.
Summary: Describes the locations and characteristics of tropical rain forests and other jungles, their animal and plant life, and their changing relationship with people.
1. Jungle ecology—Juvenile literature. 2. Rain forest ecology—Juvenile literature. [1. Jungle ecology. 2. Rain forest ecology. 3. Ecology] I. National Wildlife Federation.

QH541.5.J8W66 1986
574.5'2642 86-17966

ISBN O-912186-72-0

Acknowledgments

Jungles are among the most remote and fascinating regions on earth. Much of what we know about them comes from scientists who have spent years studying the exotic animals and plants found there. To produce this book, we drew on the help of many people with first-hand experience in jungles. At the Smithsonian Institution's National Museum of Natural History, we received generous assistance from Dr. Louise H. Emmons, Dr. Paul J. Spangler, and Addison H. Wynn. We also received information and advice from the Fish and Wildlife Service, U.S. Department of the Interior. Special thanks there are due Dr. Mercedes S. Foster, Dr. Alfred L. Gardner, Dr. Roy W. McDiarmid, Dr. Robert P. Reynolds, and Dr. Don E. Wilson. Finally, we received special help from our two scientific consultants: Dr. Ghillean T. Prance and Dr. Peter H. Raven. They reviewed each chapter of the text and offered invaluable insights into the problems facing the world's jungles today.

National Wildlife Federation

Staff for this Book

Howard F. Robinson
Editorial Director

Victor H. Waldrop
Project Editor and Writer

Bonnie S. Stutski
Photo Editor and Writer

Adele Conover
Research Editor and Writer

Donna Miller
Design Director

Vi Kirksey
Editorial Assistant

Margaret E. Wolf
Permissions Editor

Priscilla Sharpless
Paul R. Wirth
Production Managers

Pam McCoy
Production Artist

Dr. Ghillean T. Prance,
Senior Vice President for Science, Director, Institute of Economic Botany, The New York Botanical Garden

Dr. Peter H. Raven,
Director, Missouri Botanical Garden
Scientific Consultants

NATIONAL WILDLIFE FEDERATION
1412 Sixteenth Street, N.W., Washington, D.C. 20036-2266